Hal•Leonard
INSTRUMENTAL PLAY-ALONG

TRUMPET

Christmas SONGS

CONTENTS

To access audio visit:
www.halleonard.com/mylibrary

Enter Code
5381-4423-6350-0358

Audio Arrangements by Peter Deneff

ISBN 978-1-4950-2556-3

HAL•LEONARD®
CORPORATION
7777 W. BLUEMOUND RD. P.O. BOX 13819 MILWAUKEE, WI 53213

Visit Hal Leonard Online at
www.halleonard.com

ALL I WANT FOR CHRISTMAS IS YOU

TRUMPET

Words and Music by MARIAH CAREY
and WALTER AFANASIEFF

THE CHRISTMAS WALTZ

Words by SAMMY CAHN
Music by JULE STYNE

TRUMPET

HAPPY HOLIDAY

from the Motion Picture Irving Berlin's HOLIDAY INN

TRUMPET

Words and Music by
IRVING BERLIN

I WONDER AS I WANDER

TRUMPET

By JOHN JACOB NILES

I'LL BE HOME FOR CHRISTMAS

TRUMPET

Words and Music by KIM GANNON
and WALTER KENT

LET IT SNOW! LET IT SNOW! LET IT SNOW!

TRUMPET

Words by SAMMY CAHN
Music by JULE STYNE

MARY, DID YOU KNOW?

TRUMPET

Words and Music by MARK LOWRY
and BUDDY GREENE

THE MOST WONDERFUL TIME OF THE YEAR

TRUMPET

Words and Music by EDDIE POLA
and GEORGE WYLE

MY FAVORITE THINGS

from THE SOUND OF MUSIC

TRUMPET

Lyrics by OSCAR HAMMERSTEIN II
Music by RICHARD RODGERS

SILVER BELLS
from the Paramount Picture THE LEMON DROP KID

TRUMPET

Words and Music by JAY LIVINGSTON
and RAY EVANS

THIS CHRISTMAS

TRUMPET

Words and Music by DONNY HATHAWAY
and NADINE McKINNOR

WHITE CHRISTMAS

from the Motion Picture Irving Berlin's HOLIDAY INN

TRUMPET

Words and Music by
IRVING BERLIN

HAL•LEONARD INSTRUMENTAL PLAY-ALONG

Your favorite songs are arranged just for solo instrumentalists with this outstanding series. Each book includes a great full-accompaniment play-along CD so you can sound just like a pro! Check out **www.halleonard.com** to see all the titles available.

Disney Greats

Arabian Nights • Hawaiian Roller Coaster Ride • It's a Small World • Look Through My Eyes • Yo Ho (A Pirate's Life for Me) • and more.

_____ 00841934	Flute	$12.95
_____ 00841935	Clarinet	$12.95
_____ 00841936	Alto Sax	$12.95
_____ 00841937	Tenor Sax	$12.95
_____ 00841938	Trumpet	$12.95
_____ 00841939	Horn	$12.95
_____ 00841940	Trombone	$12.95
_____ 00841941	Violin	$12.95
_____ 00841942	Viola	$12.95
_____ 00841943	Cello	$12.95
_____ 00842078	Oboe	$12.95

Great Themes

Bella's Lullaby • Chariots of Fire • Get Smart • Hawaii Five-O Theme • I Love Lucy • The Odd Couple • Spanish Flea • and more.

_____ 00842468	Flute	$12.99
_____ 00842469	Clarinet	$12.99
_____ 00842470	Alto Sax	$12.99
_____ 00842471	Tenor Sax	$12.99
_____ 00842472	Trumpet	$12.99
_____ 00842473	Horn	$12.99
_____ 00842474	Trombone	$12.99
_____ 00842475	Violin	$12.99
_____ 00842476	Viola	$12.99
_____ 00842477	Cello	$12.99

Coldplay

Clocks • Every Teardrop Is a Waterfall • Fix You • In My Place • Lost! • Paradise • The Scientist • Speed of Sound • Trouble • Violet Hill • Viva La Vida • Yellow.

_____ 00103337	Flute	$12.99
_____ 00103338	Clarinet	$12.99
_____ 00103339	Alto Sax	$12.99
_____ 00103340	Tenor Sax	$12.99
_____ 00103341	Trumpet	$12.99
_____ 00103342	Horn	$12.99
_____ 00103343	Trombone	$12.99
_____ 00103344	Violin	$12.99
_____ 00103345	Viola	$12.99
_____ 00103346	Cello	$12.99

Popular Hits

Breakeven • Fireflies • Halo • Hey, Soul Sister • I Gotta Feeling • I'm Yours • Need You Now • Poker Face • Viva La Vida • You Belong with Me • and more.

_____ 00842511	Flute	$12.99
_____ 00842512	Clarinet	$12.99
_____ 00842513	Alto Sax	$12.99
_____ 00842514	Tenor Sax	$12.99
_____ 00842515	Trumpet	$12.99
_____ 00842516	Horn	$12.99
_____ 00842517	Trombone	$12.99
_____ 00842518	Violin	$12.99
_____ 00842519	Viola	$12.99
_____ 00842520	Cello	$12.99

Lennon & McCartney Favorites

All You Need Is Love • A Hard Day's Night • Here, There and Everywhere • Hey Jude • Let It Be • Nowhere Man • Penny Lane • She Loves You • When I'm Sixty-Four • and more.

_____ 00842600	Flute	$12.99
_____ 00842601	Clarinet	$12.99
_____ 00842602	Alto Sax	$12.99
_____ 00842603	Tenor Sax	$12.99
_____ 00842604	Trumpet	$12.99
_____ 00842605	Horn	$12.99
_____ 00842606	Trombone	$12.99
_____ 00842607	Violin	$12.99
_____ 00842608	Viola	$12.99
_____ 00842609	Cello	$12.99

Women of Pop

Bad Romance • Jar of Hearts • Mean • My Life Would Suck Without You • Our Song • Rolling in the Deep • Single Ladies (Put a Ring on It) • Teenage Dream • and more.

_____ 00842650	Flute	$12.99
_____ 00842651	Clarinet	$12.99
_____ 00842652	Alto Sax	$12.99
_____ 00842653	Tenor Sax	$12.99
_____ 00842654	Trumpet	$12.99
_____ 00842655	Horn	$12.99
_____ 00842656	Trombone	$12.99
_____ 00842657	Violin	$12.99
_____ 00842658	Viola	$12.99
_____ 00842659	Cello	$12.99

Movie Music

And All That Jazz • Come What May • I Am a Man of Constant Sorrow • I Believe I Can Fly • I Walk the Line • Seasons of Love • Theme from *Spider Man* • and more.

_____ 00842090	Clarinet	$10.95
_____ 00842091	Alto Sax	$10.95
_____ 00842092	Tenor Sax	$10.95
_____ 00842094	Horn	$10.95
_____ 00842095	Trombone	$10.95
_____ 00842096	Violin	$10.95
_____ 00842097	Viola	$10.95

TV Favorites

The Addams Family Theme • The Brady Bunch • Green Acres Theme • Happy Days • Johnny's Theme • Linus and Lucy • Theme from the Simpsons • and more.

_____ 00842079	Flute	$10.95
_____ 00842080	Clarinet	$10.95
_____ 00842081	Alto Sax	$10.95
_____ 00842082	Tenor Sax	$10.95
_____ 00842083	Trumpet	$10.95
_____ 00842084	Horn	$10.95
_____ 00842085	Trombone	$10.95
_____ 00842087	Viola	$10.95

Wicked

As Long As You're Mine • Dancing Through Life • Defying Gravity • For Good • I'm Not That Girl • Popular • The Wizard and I • and more.

_____ 00842236	Flute	$11.95
_____ 00842237	Clarinet	$11.95
_____ 00842238	Alto Saxophone	$11.95
_____ 00842239	Tenor Saxophone	$11.95
_____ 00842240	Trumpet	$11.95
_____ 00842241	Horn	$11.95
_____ 00842242	Trombone	$11.95
_____ 00842243	Violin	$11.95
_____ 00842244	Viola	$11.95
_____ 00842245	Cello	$11.95

FOR MORE INFORMATION, SEE YOUR LOCAL MUSIC DEALER, OR WRITE TO:

HAL•LEONARD® CORPORATION

7777 W. BLUEMOUND RD. P.O. BOX 13819 MILWAUKEE, WI 53213

Prices, contents, and availability subject to change without notice.
Disney characters and artwork © Disney Enterprises, Inc.

0315